POETRY & PROCESS

GOD INSPIRED POETRY FOR THE CALLED

BY DANA AZALIA

Poetry & Process: God inspired poetry for the called by Dana Azalia
www.creativesinnovate.com
Contact the author at creativesinnovate@gmail.com

Copyright © 2019 by Dana A. Spence All rights reserved. This book or any portion thereof may not be reproduced or used in any manner, whatsoever, without the express written permission of the publisher except for the use of brief quotations in a book review.

Scripture quotations taken from the King James Version of the Bible.

ISBN 978-0-578-71289-5

Dedication

To those that are experiencing the discipline of being processed, whether in the beginning, the middle, repeated, or the end of a process. To the ones that have difficulty identifying what you were created to do in the earth, keep seeking answers in Abba. You are the true pioneer of the new...

Table Of Contents

Introduction	09
The More	11
To Be Honest	15
Spiritual Resus	19
Show me the way to go	21
Easier	23
Where art thou	27
Nights like this	29
Synchronization	31
A Brewing	33
Purge Me	35
Meantime	37
Vindicate Me, Vindicate Us	39
What day?	41
The persistence of the pull	43
Billboards	45
I Still Love You	47
The Last to Promote	49
Only Choice	51
The Road to becoming whole	53
At your Service	55
I'm not crazy	57

I am empty again	59
Is it time to come out yet?	61
Prophets I prayed for you	63
A Process	65
A Hidden People	67
The One	69
Delusional Boxes	71
The Frontline	73
Consuming Fire (Haiku)	75
Robust Rattling	77
A New Sound	79
Wide Open	81
Deliver me from myself	83
Teatime and Worship	85

Introduction

Process... A word that is the least favorite of many, yet no one is exempt from it. Accelerated or lengthy, we all encounter Process. Entertain the thought of a deeper, unidentifiable process. There is a kind of process that we are terrible at predicting specific turns, roadblocks, and outcomes. Have you ever carried the feeling or sensing that there is more? An instant realization, an awakening, to the cycle you have been present in for years. Often, the beginning of any process is the existence of an issue or problem of some sort. Whether you are aware or not, one will begin to realize that there must be more to life than one's dreadful routine. Some may explain it as a light bulb turning on, named "Epiphany." Whatever your current state of awareness, your insides are screaming, THERE HAS TO BE MORE!" Surely the present state of being is not the end. I welcome you to the beginning of Process. The importance is not necessarily the level or subject; it is the slightest indication that Process is happening to you right now. At this very moment! It could be finding yourself doing the exact same thing in the exact same month, as the last 5 years. It could be failed relationships with the common denominator of you, coupled with familiar traits in another. It could be the end of support by trusted leadership. It could be the same blessing with a cap on it, never experiencing abundance. It could be your career or education. It could be lack of growth, or family feuds that arise at a repeated season. Whatever, and however the light bulb moments manifest, it is the impression of a divine appointment. You do not have to know exactly how to vocalize what is happening but be a willing vessel of The Creator to illustrate it through you. The key is in your, Yes! The purpose of this book is simple. I am giving artistic language to the many phases and experiences during The Process. An expression of what you feel, but cannot quite articulate at times, the definitive vision of the day to day process.

Those of you entering, or amid a season of being processed. This is your prolific hour and it is time to rise. There is a beauty in walking it out, the day to day. Many of us are entering a journey with God. The average person experiences many processes each day. There is a process for driving to a destination, getting dressed in the morning, night routines, educational progression, career succession, carrying and delivering babies, etc. I am praying that you come forth today, and without delay!!! Manifest the promises of God! The very thing that was strategically placed in your blood line as he conceived you to birth His plans into the earth. TODAY! Like Paul told Timothy, today I stir up the gift of God that is in you. *"Wherefore I put thee in remembrance that thou stir up the gift of God, which is in thee by the putting on of my hands." (2Timothy 1:6)* I exclusively invite you to "Poetry & Process", the voice of the deep during process. Enjoy and Be Blessed.

Dana Azalia

The More

What is this "MORE?"
"THE MORE?"
In the very depths of my soul
There is MORE
Caged like a bird,
Whose original intentions were never to be caged,
A breach in the Creator's original intent
Waiting for the appointed time of release
THE MORE…
Stifled by opposition, resistance
A BREACH, I SAY!
Searching for the key to unlock
THE MORE!
"You have something," he said.
"But there is no one to preserve it."
Wrestling for the release of THE MORE
How do you obtain such a thing?
I DESIRE THE TANGIBLE RELEASE OF THE MORE!
THE MORE.
How do I end this torture of THE MORE?
Clueless and questionable mindsets and position
I want to drink of THE MORE
Spreading wings like an eagle,

Soaring at record braking heights
Oh, how I can taste THE MORE
In the pit of my belly
I feel the whispers of the depths of THE MORE
Contractions are getting closer together
A growing frequency of kicks on the inside of my womb
How do I birth THE MORE?
Everything points to the suggested solution of aborting
The torture of THE MORE
Yet I feel the rhythm of every heartbeat
How do I release THE MORE?
I can sense THE MORE
It won't go away
It won't leave me alone
What must I do with the existence of THE MORE?

LORD: *Oh, but will you hunt for this?*
Will you pursue it, when it doesn't pursue you?
Will you nurture it, when it doesn't embrace you back?
Will you feed it before you feed you?
Will you focus, when it has overlooked you?
Will you love, when it appears you've been forgotten?
Will you sing of an open heaven, even when the heavens appear shut?

Dana Azalia

I replied: Yes, My Lord, I will pursue THE MORE,
when it doesn't pursue me.
I will hunt for THE MORE,
when it's hidden places seem too difficult to locate.
I will embrace THE MORE with a sweet embrace,
even when I can't feel its touch.
I will eat last to ensure its proper nourishment first.
I will focus, when it seems THE MORE has overlooked me.
I will love as Christ loves, even when the world hates me first.
I will sing of an open heaven, even when the heavens appear shut.

Note to you from the Lord: JOURNEY with me as I unlock THE MORE inside of you, waiting for a release of divine connection. I UNLOCK the ancient treasure and wake up the dormant inside of you. I prophesy, your days of hitting brick walls, ceilings, and living in a glass house are over. I release to you the capacity to DO MORE, KNOW MORE, LIVE IN THE MORE, AND EXPERIENCE THE MORE OF GOD. There. Is. More. And today you will know the secret of THE MORE.

Poetry & Process

Dana Azalia

To Be Honest

You do not always get the relief you seek,
In the form you desire
To Be Honest
Sometimes you don't get to feel better (in the flesh)
After you cried your eyes out to the Lord,
On the floor,
On your face.
Sometimes you don't get to see
Before you believe
To Be Honest
To Be Honest
To see the soothing visions of your brethren,
Before you believe.
But Believe!
Sometimes you must ask the hard questions
Before receiving the Hard Truth
Hard questions. Hard truth.
Hard questions. Hard truth.
Not your truth
But His truth
Sleepless nights
Endless attacks

While still thinking on the Lord
While still reminding yourself to thank Jesus
Sleepless nights
Endless attacks
While still repenting in case you didn't pray enough today
Sleepless nights
Endless attacks
Although, suffering was never part of your plan
It is God's plan
Sometimes you are unauthorized to know the blueprint of the plan,
Your Clearance is too low, at this time,
And yet he qualified you, STILL.
Carry out the plan.
Please do not prophesy to me, To Be Honest
I do not want another prophecy
I am enduring hardness as a good soldier
To Be Honest
To Be Honest, I still long to please The Master
Psychotic in nature
But to Be Honest
I must finish the plan
I must fulfill the call
To Be Honest
The call of an expected end
In the heart of The Father
To Be Honest
To Be Honest
To Be Honest
I still love Him

Dana Azalia

My weary eyes have not seen Him
Yet I still have to know Him
I still commune with Him
Excited for His arrival
To Be Honest
To Be Honest
To Be Honest
I STILL believe
To Be Honest
I still just have to know Him
To Be Honest
I
Still
Say
Yes.

Poetry & Process

Dana Azalia

Spiritual Resus

Spiritual Resuscitation
Revive my spirit
Dead to the old
Code blue!
Code blue!
Code blue!
Help me come to…
Help me come to…
Out of the mind
Out of the body
Call the surgeon
I cannot reach the innermost part of the soul
The people cried out for a Saul
I just want God
Exhausted resources and efforts
I just need to hook into the source
Call a code
Spiritual resus
I can't seem to catch my breath
Each time I come too…
Code blue!
Code blue!
Code blue!

Prep this one for emergency surgery
There are still fragments in the heart
Prep this one for the OR
Code blue!
Code blue!
Code blue!
Help me come to…
Help me come too…
There is a vacuum in the heart
It must come out
Spiritual Resus
Revive me
Purge me
Call a code
Help me come too…
Help me come too...
Code blue.
Code blue.

Dana Azalia

Show me the way to go

Show me the way to go
Show me the way to go
Show me the way to go
Show me the way to goo
For I do not know the way to go
So, show me the way to go
Too many forks in the road
Crying out
Show me the way to go
Too many false guides
Whispering lies
Wishing to alternate our destiny
Oh, show me the way to go
So, show me the way to go
Show me the way to go
Yesterday's frustrations cannot decide
Show me the way to go
Precious Lord, show me the way to go

Poetry & Process

Dana Azalia

Easier

Thought it would be easier by now
Died to the flesh
Excuse me, dying to the flesh
Over and over again
And when it is not enough
I died some more
Dead man walking
Just call me dead man walking
Did you die today?
Because I did
Do you tithe?
Did you sow?
Have you scattered seed in the ground?
I tithe
I sow
I scattered seed in the ground for years
Days is nonsense, years
Thought it would be easier by now
I thought the issue would be dried up by now
Like the woman with the issue of blood
An issue of 12 years dried up in an instant
Let me touch the garments of My Savior
I thought it would be easier by now

Where is the fruit of my labor?
What happened?
You said that you will know them by their fruits.
I have no fruit
Where is the fruit?
No fruit to show
Am I cursed?
You said give a tree a year to grow
Give a tree a year to grow
Years have passed
I thought by now the affirmation would manifest
Decrees and declarations
Followed by delayed manifestations
Thought by now it would be easier
But I digress
Back to the quiet place I go
Too much noise or lack thereof
I digress
I repent
Back to the closet
Embedded tears and groans
Whaling in the floor
I digress back to worship I go
Thanksgiving and praises
Worship and whaling
Prayer and fasting
I digress
Back to His presence I go
Perspective realignment

Dana Azalia

I thought it would be easier by now
But I digress
Back to His presence I go

Poetry & Process

Dana Azalia

Where art thou

Where art thou
Need your help
Need your help
Spoke your name
Just like you said
Now what?
How do I rest?
Where art thou?
I called your name
Just like you said
Where art thou?
You said you'd come
Calling your name
Just as you said
Make it stop Father
I want to rest in you

Poetry & Process

Dana Azalia

Nights like this

Nights like this
Tonight, I just want to lay in my Father's lap and cry
Let me never forget how you took your time with me
Let me never forget how your love pierced through the darkest places
Chased me down
You rescued me from the deepest valleys
The valleys I once accepted as fate
Nights like this
I cry.
For no reason at all
My only reason is all
Leave me in the lap of my Father
I care not to understand
For you to understand
Nights like this
Beyond fatigue
Sleep is distant
My Father's lap is near
Leave me here
Console me
Love me more and more
Never leave me
Never be absent like the old

Nights like this
Help me climb into your lap
I just want to cry
My Father
My Poppa
My Abba

Dana Azalia

Synchronization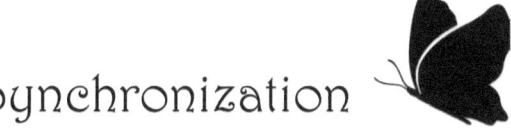

My heart in sync with His
Worthier than the worthiest
Jesus is worth every test
Perfect synchronization
Nothing short of a love illustration
Never obsolete
Freshness in the outpour of the refreshing rainfall
Remaining still to absorb each drop
All of nature obeys
Falling in line with the being of God
Never straying from the original instructions
Synchronization from the first 6 days
To the last days
Sharing the same space in time
He is mine
He is in me
I am in him
Couldn't tell us apart if you tried
One with the Father
The Father one in me

Poetry & Process

Dana Azalia

A Brewing

I feel a brewing
So much to release
Difficult to contain
Not even the walls of the church can hold this
Carry a thing
I feel a brewing
It is almost time
It is brewing
I feel a brewing
I can hardly contain it
The walls would cut its glory
It's brewing
The time is near
No, it is here
Brewing.
Daily infusions from Holy Spirit
I thought I was minding my business
Daily infusions
The drink is being prepared to perfection
Production is evident
It cannot be contained
I feel something
Like a brewing

It cannot be contained within the walls of the church
I feel a brewing
The walls would cut its glory
My God I feel a brewing
It is brewing
Where do I go?

Dana Azalia

Purge Me

Purge me once more
Will you wash me again?
Dip me in the well of The Blood
Wash me clean
Purge me
I washed my hands repeatedly
The residue
The residue is there
Will you purge me once more?
I know I was just here
Back for another washing
Will you purge me once more?
I need another washing
I apologize for the mess
Not too long ago, I was here
I know, I know
I was just here
Unable to hide the debris
I have to be free
Diligence in covering the marks
Wash me in the blood of the lamb
Renew my mind
Restore my soul

Poetry & Process

>
> Grant me clean hands
> A pure heart
> Purity is a necessity
> Clean every inch,
> Every stench
> Be sure to purge me once more
> Back for another washing
> Will you purge me once more?

Dana Azalia

Meantime

In the meantime
They said it was safe here
Another tainted space
Another faded grace
Another truth unable to trace
In the meantime
I am here
Desiring to be there
Not there but another place of there
What do we do in the meantime?
Time
Mean
Time
Time can be mean
False safety
Tricky kind of hope
In the meantime
Worship and wait
Worship and pray
Worship and fast
Worship and expect
Expectancy that the all seeing God knows
He delivers me from the snare of my enemies

In the meantime I know nothing else
I worship
Worship in singing, worship with speech
Worship in the meantime
Time can be mean
But in the meantime
The remedy known to me
Worship and wait
He knows
He sees
He is here

Dana Azalia

Vindicate Me, Vindicate Us

Oh, vindicate me, Oh Lord, before I do.
Enough is enough
To live this another day
My Lord, do something on our behalf
On the behalf of your people
Vindicate me, before I do
Smite the head of the enemy
Fight for me
Fight for us
Where is liberty?
Loose me from the gnashing teeth of the enemy
Those that plan my defeat
Not another day
The torture in my back
Did you hear me?
I called your name
I applied the blood
I spoke your word
Vindicate me, Oh Lord, before I do
Innocent and blameless for a while now
Waiting
Hoping
Expecting

Remaining faithful
Please vindicate me, Oh Lord
Vindicate us
The heart is in a tussle
Difficult not to desire them to choke on their word curses
Choke and die
I know, I know
Vengeance is yours, not mine
King of Glory, my only reason I have not drawn the other sword
My Love, the only reason I do not send tongues of war to their house
I desire to please My Lord
To refrain from doing what I could
Vindicate us Father, as we enter your rest
Blameless for a while
Tired. Going for cover
Entering your rest
Deal with them on my behalf,
On our behalf.
I only want to please My Lord.

Dana Azalia

What day?

What day escapes without a pleading of repentance?
A day without My Lord,
Is an eternity of starvation
Been hungry a long time
A long time
Stumbling upon a joy
Vacant for many years
My Lord saw fit
To include me in the mix
What a feeling
To be on the mind of God
He found time to ponder the details of my destiny
Find time.
How could I not find time?
A day without My Lord,
Is an eternity of starvation
I been Hungry a long time
A long time
Closer than the beating heart of my left breast
What day escapes without a pleading to the Lord?
My Lord, My Daddy, My Friend
Such a beautiful thing
You found time

Not only did you find time,
You created time
Time for little old me
My Lord created time for even you
What a joy…
Inseparable for eternity
Not a death sentence,
A life sentence
A life sentence without the period
He is my run-on sentence
Breaking grammatical rules
What day escapes without a pleading of the Lord?
Just useless dust that became useful
Once coupled with the breath of Yahweh
The breath of Yahweh blown into nostrils
Shifting me into an existence
Of a constant unveiling
How could I not make time for the one that created time?
He created time for me
What day escapes without?
None.
Let no day escape from me
I must remember
Let me always remember how He took His time with me
Created time… for me.
A day without My Lord is an eternity of starvation.
I been hungry a long time
A long time.

Dana Azalia

The persistence of the pull

The persistence of the pull
Do you feel it too?
A daily tug of my spirit
A tug serving as an alert
An alert to the more
There is more
There has to be more
A sight fueled by frustration
I cannot shake the pull
I see it in the shapes of the clouds,
The curve of the sun.
Lite, but strong.
Deeper.
Stronger.
Greater.
Standing at the door of more
Right at the door
Do you feel it too?
The pull
No natural explanation
I know. I know.
The tugging of my spirit
Alerting me to the unknown contents of more

No riches of this world to provoke a carnal convincing
But I am carrying something great.
The appointed time of release
I do not know
But ahhh…
The pull only gets stronger
It will not leave me be
He is there, He is here
Everywhere I go
Impossible to ignore
I am graced with the persistency of the pull
A constant tugging in my spirit

Dana Azalia

Billboards

Gray clouds posted across the sky
Damp dark grounds
Fog crowds the atmospheric fictitious world
Innumerable, we seem to lose count
A day like this
I dread the words that
Manifest like billboards in the mind
The sign reads:
IS IT REALLY, EVER GOING TO HAPPEN?
It has been near for years
IS IT REALLY, EVER GOING TO HAPPEN?
I dread the billboards of the mind
Bolder than the current state of the tongue
A day like this
Injustice is unbearable
The beatings of this place
Soon to be replaced
Brushing it aside
Knocking it out of the mind
"Let this mind be in you, which was also in Christ Jesus (Philippians 2:5)"
"Let this mind be in you, which was also in Christ Jesus (Philippians 2:5)"
"Let this mind be in you, which was also in Christ Jesus (Philippians 2:5)"
The presence of the higher one

Only The Sovereign knows
Forgive us, for you endured the worst of this place
Sent warning that "if they hate you, remember they hated me first"
Renew my mind daily
Renew my mind
I cannot stand the billboard of the current state of this day
Change my mind
Through you I rewrite the billboards of the mind
The narrative must change

Dana Azalia

I Still Love You

At 3:39 AM I confess my love for you again.
I still love you
I still believe
I only know your plans for me must be good
I know not the specifics,
The steps in the road to higher
I only know your plans for me are good, it is of hope, it is of an expected end (Jeremiah 29:11)
Even in the agony,
The clouds of confusion,
There is one thing I am never confused about;
I still love you Yahweh
King of Glory, I still believe
Any day now,
In the blink of an eye
All things are possible
All things.
I still love you.

Poetry & Process

Dana Azalia

The Last to Promote

It would dismantle the formation of my heart
To disappoint God
Help me.
To be the last to promote
The furthest from the target of desire
If I remain in His Perfect will
Not a will, but His perfect will
The core of my being longs for you more, and more
I am in you and you are in me,
A oneness that still hungers
to be embedded all the more
Closer than your omnipotent presence
Deeper than the center of the soul
If it exists, I want it
A mutual abiding beyond earthly explanation
A willing vessel
If first never graces the platform of the shoulders
Just let me remain in the Perfect will of the Father,
closer than the borrowed breath that flows
through the bloodstream
Passing the edge of my existence
It would dismantle the formation of my heart

Poetry & Process

Dana Azalia

Only Choice

He is not my last resort
He is my only choice.
He is the door of my being
Just me and My Lord
Leave me here
Just me and My Lord
Hover over me
Usher me deeper
I want to lay in my Father's lap
Leave me here
Just me and My Lord
Generic brands, no thank you
This spot is taken and never to be replaced
I know too much
I am in too deep
Deeper than black holes hidden beyond galaxies
Billions and Billions of miles away from comprehension
He is not my last resort
He is my only choice
Set apart
The desire to mingle with corruption has ceased
Holy, Holy, Holy
Set a part

Poetry & Process

                    Just for Him
                    My only choice
                   I choose him daily

Dana Azalia

The Road to becoming whole

The road to becoming whole
Complete.
The road to becoming whole
Abba, Make me whole again
I was not always this way
Complete surrender
Enter in the house of this heart
Search every hidden place
Every corner
Every crevice
Leave no space untouched
Major repairs
Minor setbacks
Undergoing a mass construction
Responding to the call of the deep
On the road to becoming whole
Wholeness in the deep dark places
The places we like to forget The places we disassociate
The random flashbacks
The thoughts we thought were erased
On the road to becoming whole

Poetry & Process

Dana Azalia

At your Service

I am at your service
Yahweh I am at your service
In you I live
In you I have my being
I am ready
I am at your service
I do as you will
I go where you go
I say what you say
I see what you see
Yahweh I am at your service
You stood at the door and Knocked
I heard the knock
I answer the knock
At your service My Lord
Just say the word

Poetry & Process

Dana Azalia

I'm not crazy

Something has grabbed a hold of my voice
I sense the insensible
I'm not crazy
How can you not know it
Lack of eye sight yet I see
How can you not see
I promise I'm not crazy
I don't mean to compare but the contrast is not fair
Undeserving of the easy
I can't be crazy
Oh do it already
I remember the days I couldn't go up
Longing to go deeper and higher
Why the difficulty
Easy for some
Access granted but I remember the access denied
Sanctification

Poetry & Process

Dana Azalia

I am empty again

I need a fresh infilling
Refill me
Pour into me
I'm empty again
Father, it is me and I am empty again
WIll you fill me
Ahhhh I searched for a man
A man thought to be your disciple
Yet they Could not do it
Careful not to make man idol
My spirit man feels idle
I am empty again
My King, won't you fill me gain
Barren reservoirs
At your feet
Ready for another deposit
Let the waterfalls of heaven flow
I need an unconventional infilling
unconventional
Fill me

Poetry & Process

Dana Azalia

Is it time to come out yet?

Is it time to come out yet?
I've been in this old cave
For an observed eternity
Is the time near? I been thinking on some things
Things that may be irrelevant
Does the sun still shine on the outside?
Is it safe to come out?
The security clearance to move
The clearance to be.
Is it time to remove the head of the enemy?
Set apart before conception
"Daughter, you must be processed"
"I have been preparing you"
A God induced incubation
Requires seasons and years of isolation
Each time I question, is it time to come out yet?
Holy Spirit reminds me of the vision
"Can you handle being alone?"
Yes! I can handle being alone.
The book is written
Process me
Process me again and again
I can handle being alone

Put me in the gap,
At the core of the dark cold cave
It is for my good

Dana Azalia

Prophets I prayed for you

I see the plan of the massacre of the prophets
Father has revealed the burden of intercession, for His Prophets
His burden, for His Prophets
The year of the mouthpiece of God
A Danger and a safety in what you declare
Jehovah Gibbor, we need you
Drench your weapons in The Blood
Serve our predators to the beast of the wild
Prophets, I prayed for you
Let us not be deceived
I call the wind beneath your wings to thrust you higher
I speak strength in your backs,
Exercise the authority in the shoulders,
Acceleration in your feet,
I break deceit off the mind
You are the mind of God!
Be renewed!
Utilize the power in each piece of armor
Our Father has redeemed us.
Prophets, I prayed for you...

Poetry & Process

Dana Azalia

A Process

I know of a process not very kind
I know of a process beyond the mind
Troubles of consistency
Breeding consistent troubles
Of infinite accuracy
Stepping out of the venue of complacency
Shedding the skin of infancy
Thoughts of aborting the mission
Not allowed to go against the orders of the Great Physician
However long it takes
Whatever the Potter desires to make
Beyond Higher stakes
The results it breeds are divine
Intertwine my whole being to align
I know of a process not very kind
I know of a process beyond the mind

Poetry & Process

Dana Azalia

A Hidden People

There are a hidden people
Set aside for the Almighty God alone
There are a people that dare not be exposed before time
There are a people that care not for your pulpit and ministry positions
There are a people that prophesy over themselves
There are a people that just want God
I want God!
A people that will not let relatives nor friend draw a wedge between them and God
A faithful people
A greater measure
Obedient unto death
A people that will view delay of exposure as God's plan
The Perfect plan
There is a people that rise in the middle of the dark day
Deep dark places
Deep dark places
Yearning for the voice of the Lord
The presence that surpasses small expectations of the best company
There are a people waiting
A people spared
Soon you will see
In His time

Longing to bask in the purity of the unknown
A people that must be found
To set the tone of God
A people thought to be lost since the ancient days
Though In plain sight
You could not see
There are a people with a technology that can save many
There are a people that walk with God daily
A people that embrace deliverance daily
A people that carry the heartbeat of heaven

Dana Azalia

The One

The one with the least talent
I am the one with the least talent
The One called to The One
Perplexity in identifying the least
Banned abilities present to name a thing
Or the lack of
Unable to make out the picture
Pictures of the solution held in a willing vessel
The least of the wise
The least of the one
The one with the least talent
Called to The One
Permitted to mature in hiding
Wilderness living
What do I call the one with the least…?
Called to The One
The one of the ones spared
I am she
I am he
I lay in silk silhouettes of The God I have not seen
The God of him who believes
The least of these
The greatest amongst thieves

Who do you say that I am?
Well, I am the one with the least talent
Called to the One
The One who chose the least of these
Concealed amongst those thought to have prestige
In the progression of extinction
I am the one
I am the one that heeds the call to The One
The one with the least talent
Called to the One

Dana Azalia

Delusional Boxes

I call you to expand beyond delusional boxes
False Limitations
Outsiders placed upon you
Come into the very being
Of your original design
I call you to align
Imposters impose illegal pressures
The imposture is you
No "how to?"
Just do!
Be the doer
Prohibited from simply hearing
It takes years and tears
It takes isolation and transformation
It takes persistence and resilience
It takes groaning and moaning,
Kicking and screaming
Break free from delusional boxes
Only a fool will say, "It doesn't take all of that"
The incomplete wisdom of a fool
Only a fool will say, "It doesn't take all of that"
I call you to expand beyond the Delusional boxes. Delusional walls and ceilings

Poetry & Process

Forming boxes that impose illegal pressures in a no name season
Push past what others allude to as their end
A new beginning is here you

Dana Azalia

The Frontline

Put me on the frontline
I am ready
A few righteous for the preservation of a nation
Put me on the frontline
I am ready
I see a few righteous here
We are ready
We do it for you alone
We are ready
Make us ready
From the back to the front of the line
Ready to fight
I march on the head of the serpent
Because my Father says so
The army is rising
The army is rising
The army of the ONE TRUE LIVING GOD
Put me on the frontline
I am ready

Poetry & Process

Dana Azalia

Consuming Fire (Haiku)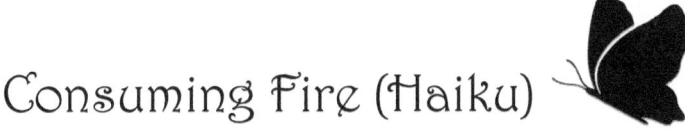

Burn impurities
Cultivate imperfections
A pure finishing

Poetry & Process

Dana Azalia

Robust Rattling

A rattling in the womb
Purpose is growing
Standing in the womb
Extending to heights in the ribcage
Rearranging vital organs
Delivery is near
The very layers of the womb
Shaking to a unique rhythm of the drum
The drums
The sound of Yah
The image of God
Exceeding spaces in the womb
Useless living
We were never created for ordinary living
Impregnated a shapeless thing
Giving it form
A vessel of love
Robust rattling
Abandoning the form of the world
Take on the appropriate form

Poetry & Process

Dana Azalia

A New Sound

A new sound to nourish the inside
I stumbled across one
That's old
That's not it
There's something else
Something fresh
I'll know when I find it
Wear it out
Until another urgency ignites
Another new sound
New sounds call for new seasons
A change in the times
The tempo of heaven
The lullaby before entrance into the canal of earth
Hungry for it
Indescribable to man
I'll know when I hear it
As it falls upon my head
Crawling into the gates of the ear
Seeping through the wall of the
An expedition to the unseen compartments of the soul
Poetic innate ability
Homesick

Gravitating to the sound of home
Frequent visits
The new sound
The sound of home
An itch that only a new sound could scratch
Morning's Original melodies singing on the branch of a tree
Newborn
State- of-the-art

Dana Azalia

Wide Open

I feel love entering the depths of the deep
Entering back into my heart
Returning to the forgotten places
Thought to be extinct
Yahweh, you dug me out of the grave
You located the root of the cause
I couldn't imagine the positioning
In the places you designed for me
Wide open
Excited for the arrival of the sacred
Open like the land of the sea
My insides sit outside of my body
The unexpected is taking place
I ran as far as my tired legs could
Vulnerability outlasted me
Wide open, indeed.

Poetry & Process

Dana Azalia

Deliver me from myself

Can two sit on one throne?
Live in me
Guilty of deliberate obstruction
My vision did not allow me to see
The beautiful function you designed me to be
Deliver me from myself
Unknowingly adopted sabotage, as a harvest of cycles
The robber of my own inheritance
Live in me,
As one again
Can two reign in one land at the same time?
Deliver me from myself

Poetry & Process

Dana Azalia

Teatime and Worship

I sip tea and worship The Creator
Teatime with my Abba
Here, peace saturates the atmosphere
In a globe less favorable
I locate the hidden door
The door of doors
Dimensions only Abba knows
Sip tea and worship
Closing my eyes to focus on Him
In me,
But around me.
On me,
But beside me.
Behind me, but in front of me.
Supernatural sensations around my head
Touching my mind
Enlighten my mind
You left the 99 to attend teatime
What's the tea?
Abba and I alone.
Ministering.
Communing.
Dine with me.

Poetry & Process

www.ingramcontent.com/pod-product-compliance
Lightning Source LLC
Chambersburg PA
CBHW021412290426
44108CB00010B/499